Janet Guthrie

Indy Car Racing Pioneer

Other titles in the Innovators series include:

INNOVATORS

Janet Guthrie

Indy Car Racing Pioneer

Barbara Sheen

KIDHAVEN PRESS
A part of Gale, Cengage Learning

GALE
CENGAGE Learning

Detroit • New York • San Francisco • New Haven, Conn • Waterville, Maine • London

LIBRARY OF CONGRESS CATALOGING-IN-PUBLICATION DATA

Sheen, Barbara.
  Janet Guthrie : Indy car racing pioneer / by Barbara Sheen.
    p. cm. -- (Innovators)
  Includes bibliographical references and index.
  ISBN 978-0-7377-5050-8 (hardcover)
  1. Guthrie, Janet, 1938---Juvenile literature. 2. Automobile racing drivers--United States--Biography--Juvenile literature. 3. Women automobile drivers--United States--Biography--Juvenile literature. I. Title.
  GV1032.G87S54 2010
  796.72092--dc22
  [B]
                                                            2009041729

KidHaven Press
27500 Drake Rd.
Farmington Hills, MI 48331

ISBN-13: 978-0-7377-5050-8
ISBN-10: 0-7377-5050-2

Printed in the United States of America
1 2 3 4 5 6 7 14 13 12 11 10

Printed by Bang Printing, Brainerd, MN, 1st Ptg., 04/2010

CONTENTS

Paving the Way

The Indianapolis 500 (Indy 500), held in Indianapolis, Indiana, is one of the toughest car races in the world. Competitors race 500 miles (805km) at speeds over 240 miles per hour (386kph) in **open-wheel cars**.

It takes a special kind of person to compete in the race. Drivers must have nerves of steel and incredible powers of concentration. They must focus on the road and be able to make split-second decisions. Their lives depend on it. They must be physically strong, too.

No Females Allowed

For most of its history, the Indy 500 has been an all male event. Many men connected with the race, and some members of the general public thought that women were not mentally or physically strong enough to compete in car races. They also believed that women were bad drivers whose participation would endanger the other drivers. In fact, until 1971, it was not just the Indy 500 track that was off-limits to women. Women were also not allowed in the press box or racing **pits**. Even the drivers' wives were banned. "A woman might be a reporter, a photographer . . . she might own a race car—but she could not get near it at any time for any reason. A woman on the track itself was unthinkable,"[1] Janet Guthrie explains.

Janet Guthrie changed how the racing world viewed women racers.

Janet Guthrie

A Courageous Woman

Janet Guthrie changed the way the racing world looked at women. In 1977 she became the first woman to compete in the Indy 500. Her performance proved that women were able to successfully compete in the race.

Getting to the Indy 500 was not easy. During her racing career, Guthrie faced insults from fans, hostility from other drivers, lack of interest from sponsors, and criticism from the press. She also was the butt of crude jokes. "I was the one who had to deal with all the cries of 'women can't do it,'"[2] she says. But Guthrie did not back down.

Today female race-car drivers are part of the racing world. In fact three women started in the 2009 Indy 500. Guthrie's courage and determination helped pave their way. "I did not set out to be a pioneer of racing," she says, "but it has been gratifying to me to see the changes that have taken place."[3]

CHAPTER 1

Where the Action Is

Janet Guthrie did not know that she would become a race-car driver. But she always loved adventure. Guthrie felt that she could do anything.

Bold Heroes

Janet Guthrie was born in Iowa City, Iowa, on March 7, 1938. She was the oldest of five children. Her mother, Jean, was a homemaker. Her father, Lain, was a pilot. The Guthries taught their children that they could do anything they put their mind to. It did not matter if a person was a boy or a girl. "I was lucky to have parents who didn't think there was any difference in bringing up their boys and girls,"[4] Guthrie says.

Guthrie was adventurous at an early age. When she was four, she learned to ride a bicycle after only one short lesson. Soon she was pedaling all over the neighborhood.

From childhood, Guthrie loved adventure stories and physical activity.

Not long after Guthrie learned to ride a bike, the family moved to an isolated, wooded area outside Miami, Florida. There were no children her age for Guthrie to play with. And there were not many paved roads to bicycle on, so Guthrie spent a lot of time reading. Her mother had taught her how.

She read about five books a week. Her favorites were adventures. At that time heroes in adventure stories were usually men or boys. That did not bother Guthrie. She imagined herself in their place—flying airplanes, sailing ships, or rocketing into outer space. It was not that she wanted to be a boy. "I just did not have any trouble identifying with the adventures boys may have. I did not see any reason why I couldn't do the same thing,"[5] she explains.

Taking Off

Guthrie started school when she was five. She attended a private school in Miami. To get to school, she walked to a small airport a mile (1.6km) away from the family home. Once there she boarded an airport limousine. It took her to a public bus stop 5 miles (8km) away in South Miami. Guthrie then waited for the bus, which took her to the school. She repeated the whole trip in reverse when school was over each day. Her mother made the

Flying became Guthrie's passion and her father gave her flying lessons when she was thirteen.

journey with her the first few times. After that, Guthrie was on her own. Getting to and from school might have frightened a less-daring child. But it did not faze Guthrie. She had imagined herself taking much longer and more dangerous journeys many times. Once, when she was six years old, the airport limousine failed to pick her up at the bus stop. Guthrie started walking the whole 6 miles (9.7km) home by herself. Her parents found her after she had gone about halfway. She did not understand why they were worried. To a child that pictured herself slaying dragons, the hike seemed harmless.

School was yet another adventure. Guthrie was a good student. In fact, because she could read when she started school, she was put in the second grade when she was five years old. But school alone was not exciting enough to satisfy Guthrie. Her favorite adventure books were about flying and Guthrie wanted to learn to fly an airplane. Her father often took her flying with him. She begged her father to teach her.

When she was thirteen, he gave in. "I would beg to go flying, my father would instruct. I'd do things wrong, he'd yell angrily. I'd cry. When I got over it, I would beg to go flying again,"[6] she explains.

Flying became Guthrie's first passion. She loved soaring through the air. She loved the feeling of speed and control. She flew **solo** for the first time when she was sixteen. A year later she got her pilot's license.

Parachute Jumping

The same year that Guthrie got her pilot's license, she read pilot Charles Lindbergh's autobiography. In it he writes about parachute jumping. Guthrie imagined herself in Lindbergh's

Guthrie studied parachute jumping and jumped from a plane only one time.

shoes. She nagged her father to let her try. Unlike today, there were no training schools for parachute jumping. So a retired air show entertainer showed Guthrie how to handle a parachute. He taught her how to put it on, how to pull the **rip cord**, and how to land on the ground. She practiced by jumping off the roof of her house.

Impressed with her determination, her father decided to let her make an actual jump, but only if he flew the plane. This was a very dangerous adventure. If something went wrong, she could be killed. Would she have the courage to step out of the plane into thin air?

When the time came, Guthrie did not hesitate. It was an awesome experience, silent and beautiful. But she never did it again. She did it just once so she could experience what it was like, but she was not interested in doing it again. According to Guthrie, she had "pressed the limits of experience."[7] Now she was ready for new challenges.

A Mental Adventure

Guthrie graduated from high school a year later in 1955. She was seventeen years old. She would have liked to join the U.S. Air Force and become a pilot. But women were not yet allowed to fly military airplanes. She could not become a commercial airline pilot either. The airlines did not hire female pilots. Instead she went to the University of Michigan, where she studied **physics**.

It was rare for a woman to study physics. But Guthrie did not let that stop her. She loved the subject. It was, she says, "an adventure for the mind."[8]

Although there were few women in her physics classes, Guthrie was not afraid to be different. "I used to ask myself, 'Why am I involved in these men's activities?'" she says. "Then I realized that they're . . . exciting . . . I've always enjoyed challenges."[9]

Studying physics was not Guthrie's only challenge. In her spare time, she continued flying. She put in over 400 hours in the air and got her commercial pilot's license when she was nineteen. She also became a licensed flight instructor. She could fly twenty different kinds of airplanes. When she graduated from the University of Michigan in 1960, she was ready to try something new. Her life as a scientist was about to begin.

CHAPTER 2

Fast and Ferocious

After graduating from college, Janet Guthrie was not sure where life would lead her. She hoped to marry and have a family someday, but she was not yet ready to settle down. She was eager to have new and exciting adventures on the ground and in the air.

Aiming for the Moon

Guthrie took a job as an engineer with Republic Aviation in Long Island, New York. She worked in the company's research center on Project Fire, which contributed to the development of the rockets that were flown to the moon. She loved the mental challenge, but she missed the thrill of flying.

In 1964 the National Aeronautics and Space Administration (NASA) started a program in which they trained scientists to become astronauts. It seemed like the perfect job for Guthrie. She had dreamed of exploring space when she was a little girl.

Now she might actually get a chance. "It was the great adventure of the twentieth century," she says. "Sure I wanted to be out there in the last Frontier. Who wouldn't?"[10]

She scored high on the academic tests NASA required, becoming one of only four women who made it to the second round of evaluations. But, in the end, she was not chosen. NASA wanted people with advanced college degrees.

Sleek and Beautiful

Guthrie was disappointed. She considered going to school at night to earn a doctorate degree. Doing so, however, would interfere with another interest that she had recently developed, sports-car driving. When she was a teenager, she was given a chance to drive a Jaguar XK-120 owned by a friend of her family. It was a sleek, fast sports car. Guthrie thought it was the most

Guthrie was passionate about cars and bought a gray Jaguar XK-120 similar to this one.

beautiful car she had ever seen. She vowed that she would own one someday. When she spotted an ad for a used Jaguar XK-120, she had to decide whether to buy it or spend her money on a partial share in a small airplane. Once she looked at the car, she had to have it. Her decision was made.

She did not know it at the time, but that decision changed her life. Racing was about to replace flying as her great passion. "I made a choice that proved to be a watershed in my life, a Continental Divide, of greater import than I could have dreamed," she says. "The gray Jaguar . . . was irresistible."[11]

Competing

At first Guthrie used her Jaguar for transportation. It was not long before she joined a local sports-car club and got involved in **gymkhanas**. A gymkhana is an amateur contest of driving skill in which competitors drive in a zigzag pattern between rubber cones. The driver who finishes the course fastest and hits the fewest cones is the winner. Guthrie was a natural. Within a few months, she was named the female gymkhana champion of Long Island.

Guthrie then began competing in **hill-climbing races**. In this type of race, drivers competed, one car at a time, on winding mountain roads. The driver who finished the race fastest was the winner. These races were popular in the 1950s and 1960s. It was not uncommon for a driver to mishandle a turn, fly off the road, and plummet down the side of the mountain. In one race that Guthrie competed in another driver was almost killed. That did not scare Guthrie or cause her to lose focus. She recalls that the news of what happened just made her drive

Hill-climbing races can be extremely dangerous since the cars are driven so close to the edges of mountain cliffs.

more cautiously on the part of the course where the other driver had lost control of his car. Years later she realized that her reaction was typical of a competitive race-car driver.

"This Racing Was Ferocious"

It was not long before Guthrie wanted to try something even more challenging—sports-car road racing. In these amateur races, drivers race against each other at speeds exceeding 100 miles per hour (161kph). They race on specially constructed, closed-circuit tracks that have turns and hills just like the open road. Guthrie attended a special driving school to get a sports-car racing license.

After two days of practice, the students got to race against each other. Guthrie had never had so much fun. Even flying was not this exciting. Being able to compete fender to fender against the other drivers and watch them in her mirror as she whizzed past them was thrilling. And knowing that any mistake could have serious consequences, made it all the more exciting. "This racing was ferocious! I loved it!"[12] she explains.

Guthrie finished third in the race at the driving school. She got a silver bowl for her performance. She also earned her sports-car racing license. At that moment she recalls, "The whole racing world lay waiting."[13]

Auto Mechanic

Now that she had her license, Guthrie was eager to start entering sports-car races. Her Jaguar XK-120 was fine for gymkhanas and hill climbing, but it was not fast enough for sports-car racing. She needed a more powerful car. In 1963 she bought a used Jaguar XK-140. Race cars take a lot of abuse. They need constant maintenance. Guthrie could not afford a mechanic to care for the car, so she decided she would work on it herself.

She knew very little about auto mechanics. The best way to

Guthrie learned about the Jaguar's engine by taking it apart, studying it, and then rebuilding it.

learn, she thought, was to take the Jaguar's engine apart, study every piece, then put it back together.

She used an abandoned barn for a garage. It had no electricity or heat. Using a flashlight to see and the Jaguar's repair manual for guidance, she gradually disassembled then reassembled the car's engine.

It was hard and dirty work. The barn was freezing cold, and she did not have the right tools. But she did not quit. It took her three long months, working every night. When she was

finished, she knew as much about a race-car's engine as most mechanics. Now she was ready to race.

She drove in twelve sports-car races in 1964, including a 500-mile (805km) race in Watkins Glen, New York. Competing against 39 other cars, some driven by well-known drivers, Guthrie placed sixth. That was fantastic for a new driver. And it was just the beginning.

CHAPTER 3

Running on Empty

More and more, racing was taking over Janet Guthrie's life. She did not plan on becoming a professional race-car driver. It happened gradually. She knew it was impractical. But the thrill of racing was hard to resist.

Macmillan Ring-Free Oil

In 1966 Guthrie's racing record caught the attention of the Macmillan Ring-Free Oil Company. It was putting together a team of five female drivers to drive their two race cars. They wanted Guthrie to be a part of the team, which was called the Macmillan Motor Maids.

Their first race was the Daytona Continental, a 24-hour endurance race. The team was given Sunbeam Alpines, small, low-powered cars that were no competition for the more powerful vehicles in the race. Guthrie drove one Sunbeam, alternating with two other team members behind the wheel.

Guthrie, center, with her team of female drivers, wait to participate in the annual Sebring endurance race in May 1969.

While many teams dropped out, the car driven by Janet's team and the other Macmillan car co-driven by the two other Motor Maids, finished the race. Guthrie's car came in 31st, which was a major accomplishment. According to Guthrie, "driving a little rat of a car, where you have to keep an eye out behind you and in front of you is more difficult than driving one of the faster cars."[14]

The team raced once or twice a year for the next few years. In the second year, Guthrie finished twelfth in Daytona. And, in a difficult twelve-hour race in Sebring, Florida, she finished second among the cars in her class, which means she finished second among cars of similar power to the car she was driving, By 1971, she had a record of finishing nine races in a row in some of the toughest endurance races in the United States and two first-in-class finishes at Sebring, which is known for its rough course, that includes seventeen turns.

Looking for Sponsors

Guthrie's involvement with racing was becoming more and more intense. In 1967 Republic Aviation closed down. Janet was out of work. At the time, she still considered herself an amateur driver who, she says, "was racing for the love of it."[15] But she did not take another job. Instead, she raced in her Jaguar whenever she could.

By 1968, the Jaguar was too old to race. So she sold it. Even with the money from selling her car, Guthrie's money was dwindling, so she took a job as a technical editor for Sperry Rand, an electronics and computer manufacturer. Now without a race car, Guthrie also looked for a sponsor. Since racing can cost thousands of dollars, drivers need a sponsor, like a race-car owner or a corporation, who will pay for a top-quality car, mechanics, and other expenses. In return, race-car owners get prize money when their car wins a race. Corporations get free advertising. Their product's name is printed on drivers' uniforms and on the sides of their cars. Guthrie sent out dozens of letters and went to racetracks to talk to car owners in hopes of finding a sponsor. No one wanted to take a chance on her.

Her friends encouraged her to give up her quest, but she refused. "I never stopped looking for a ride, sending out sponsorship proposals, trying to find my way into the seat of any race car I could,"[16] she explains.

Building Her Own Car

Since no one was willing to sponsor Guthrie, she decided to build her own race car. In 1972 she bought a Toyota Celica, which she tore apart. Bit by bit, she replaced each part with one that would

Despite success at regional races, Guthrie could not find a sponsor.

power a race car. She spent every cent she had on the car. It was
at this point that she set out to be a professional race-car driver.

She raced the car in a series of regional races held in the
Northeastern part of the United States and racked up an im-
pressive record, including becoming the North Atlantic Road
Racing Champion. A New York Toyota dealer helped her with
expenses. But, if she was going to succeed on a national level,
she needed a national sponsor. She created a proposal for car
manufacturer Toyota USA to sponsor her. She flew to California to present the proposal to Toyota's national representatives.
They listened politely then turned her down.

Opportunity Knocks

Guthrie quit her technical editing job and took a series of odd
jobs to support herself. She continued racing the Toyota whenever she could. It was a bad time for Guthrie. "I had no house, no
jewelry, no insurance, no husband, no savings. I was in debt. I
had one used up race car. And I was saying to myself, 'You really
must come to your senses,'"[17] she recalls. That meant giving up
her dream. The very thought felt like death.

Then in 1976 she finally got her chance. Rolla Vollstedt,
a racing team owner, asked Guthrie to join his team for the
1976 Indy 500. Guthrie had limited experience driving an
open-wheel car on a large oval track. To make sure she was
comfortable with this type of driving, she agreed to a test drive
in Ontario, California.

Two weeks before the test drive she broke her foot. Her
doctor put her in a plaster cast from her toes to her knee. The
doctor said Guthrie could not drive. But she had worked too
hard to let a broken bone stop her.

Guthrie looking disappointed after failing to finish the Trenton 200 in 1976 because of engine trouble.

The night before the test drive, she removed the cast by soaking it in the bathtub. She arrived for the test without her crutches, telling Vollstedt that her limp was caused by a twisted ankle. When she got into the test car, she had no idea whether she would be able operate the brake with her broken foot. She knew that she was going to try.

Guthrie was able to operate the brake. She aced the test drive. And she loved the experience. She says driving such a powerful car made her feel like "I had a tiger by the tail."[18] But the path to the Indy 500 was still littered with obstacles. There was a lot of publicity about her now and a lot of opposition to a female Indy driver. Some of the male drivers were harsh. For example, driver Bobby Unser said that he could teach a male hitchhiker to drive better than Guthrie. Driver Johnny Parsons Jr. said that because of her inability due to being female, Guthrie would put the other drivers in the hospital.

The press and many racing fans were also unkind. Guthrie tried to ignore the uproar. "What really mattered was what happened on the track,"[19] she says. Here, she was splendid.

She drove in the Trenton 200, a professional open-wheel race. Although engine trouble kept her from finishing the race, she came in 50th out of a field of 29 cars. Mechanical trouble also kept her from winning a place in the 1976 Indy 500. She did get to do a practice run in a car owned by racing legend, A.J. Foyt. She drove that car at a speed that would have qualified her for the race if Foyt had asked her to join his team. But he did not. Her Indy dreams were over for that year, but there were still other races to run.

CHAPTER 4

NASCAR, Indy, and Beyond

Janet Guthrie had come closer than any woman in history to competing in the Indy 500. But, coming close was not enough for her. She would try again. In the meantime, a new adventure awaited her.

NASCAR

Guthrie's attempt to win a starting position in the Indy 500 caught the attention of Lynda Ferrari, a North Carolina banker. She had recently bought a race car and recruited a corporate sponsor. She invited Guthrie to drive the car in the Charlotte 600. At 600 miles (966km), it is the longest of all NASCAR (National Association for Stock Car Auto Racing) races. In NASCAR racing, **stock cars**, which are standard passenger cars modified for professional racing, are raced on **banked** oval tracks known as **superspeedways**.

By the end of the 1977 NASCAR Winston Cup series, Guthrie had ten finishes in the top twelve.

Guthrie jumped on the opportunity. Not surprisingly, she faced the same kind of hostility in Charlotte, North Carolina, as she had in Indianapolis, Indiana. Although other women had driven in the early days of NASCAR racing, which had its first official race in 1949, none had competed in a race over 200 miles (322km).

The fact that driving a stock car was fairly new for Guthrie added to the negativity that the press and male drivers had. But she was confident she could handle the car. "I had a very strong desire," she explains. "So I was able to grab the opportunity with both hands and the long toes of my feet and make the most of it."[20]

Not only did Guthrie **qualify**, she placed fifteenth in the race. Her performance earned her the Curtin Turner Award for outstanding accomplishment on the track.

She continued to race in NASCAR's Winston Cup series, a group of 31 races run by NASCAR. By the end of 1977, she had ten finishes in the top twelve. At one point, she was in the lead at a race at Ontario Motor Speedway in Ontario, California. And the next year, she finished sixth at the Bristol Motor Speedway in Bristol, Tennessee, racing on a high-banked track that makes the race one of NASCAR's most difficult. "There is nothing like Bristol," she says. "It's like a teacup for a giant. . . . Boy was it fun."[21]

Back to Indianapolis

NASCAR driving was great, but Guthrie still wanted to prove herself at the Indy 500. In 1977 she again joined Rolla Vollstedt's team. On the first day of practice, she posted the fastest speed on the track. Three days later, she remained among the top-ten fastest cars.

When Guthrie's car was damaged during a practice drive, it looked like she would not get a chance to make a qualifying run. But the car was fixed just in the nick of time for her to try for a spot in the race. Still, there was a possibility that the car would break down during the qualifying run. Guthrie recalls, "The question was simply: Would the engine last? . . . I was holding my breath . . . had the engine blown . . . that was it."[22]

The car made it, and Guthrie qualified to race in the Indy 500. She was the first woman to ever qualify for the prestigious race.

Guthrie is applauded by her crew after she became the first woman to qualify for the Indy 500 in May 1977.

On the day of the race after track owner Tony Hulman announced, "in the company with the first lady ever to qualify for Indianapolis, gentlemen, start your engines."[23] But luck was not with Guthrie.

Early on her car had mechanical problems. At one point, fuel spilled into the cockpit and seeped into her driving suit. Although it burned her, she kept driving. But her car would not cooperate. After 27 laps, mechanical problems forced her to drop out.

Making History Again

After her showing in 1977, Guthrie was confident that she would be offered a ride in the 1978 Indy 500. Vollstedt was not sponsoring a team that year. So Guthrie contacted other race-team owners. But no offers came. Guthrie was one of the most famous race-car drivers around, yet she had no ride.

She did not give up. Since no one would offer her a ride, she created her own Indy team. This meant she had to buy a car, hire and manage a crew, and drive. But first she had to find someone to pay for it. She contacted dozens of corporate sponsors. No one was interested.

Sponsored by Texaco in 1978, Guthrie finished ninth in the Indy 500.

Then one month before the race, the oil company, Texaco, agreed to fund her. They gave her about $115,000, which was about 5 percent of the budget of most racing teams. But it was a chance, and Guthrie grabbed it.

With little time to spare, she managed to get a car and a crew. The car was not the most powerful on the track, but Guthrie got the best out of it. She earned a starting place in the race on the first day of qualifying.

Then two days before the race, she broke her wrist. With a broken wrist, it would be difficult to shift gears. Other drivers might have given up. Guthrie found a doctor who numbed the wrist with medication so she could drive.

And drive she did. She finished ninth. For the next 27 years, this was the best finish by any woman in the Indy 500. (Danica Patrick finished fourth in 2005.) She did it with limited resources, and a crew she managed herself. It was an incredible achievement.

And Beyond

Guthrie's success earned her the respect of the other drivers. But it did not get her a sponsor who would put her in a winning car. Her last race was the 1980 Daytona 500. That same year she was inducted into the International Women's Sports Hall of Fame in New York, New York.

She kept searching for a ride until 1983. Finally out of frustration, she retired. In all, she competed in 33 NASCAR races and 11 Indy races. She would have liked to compete in more. "I didn't quit willingly," she explains. "I wish I could have competed enough to prove that women aren't only competitive, but

Guthrie was inducted into the International Motor Sports Hall of Fame in 2006.

can win. Without money, you're just a fast pedestrian. I would have loved to continue racing."[24]

In the years after she retired, Guthrie moved to Colorado, where she married an airline pilot. Her racing suit and helmet are on display in the Smithsonian Institute in Washington, D.C. In 2006 she was inducted into the International Motorsports Hall of Fame & Museum in Talladega, Alabama.

Guthrie became a popular public speaker and a driving safety expert. And she wrote *Janet Guthrie: A Life at Full Throttle*, a best-selling book about her life. It took her more than twenty years to complete it. She hopes that her story makes the public more aware of the role women have played in the history of motor sports and makes it easier for others to dare to be different.

NOTES

Introduction: Paving the Way

1. Quoted in Dave Caldwell, "Racing to Victory, and Leaving the Men and the Doubters Behind," *New York Times*, April 21, 2008, www.nytimes.com/2008/04/21/sports/othersports/21patrick.html?_r=3&scp=2&sq=danica+patrick&st=nyt&oref=slogin.

2. Quoted in Brandon George, "Pioneer Janet Guthrie Takes a Victory Lap," *Dallas News*, June 5, 2005.

3. Quoted in George, "Pioneer Janet Guthrie Takes a Victory Lap."

Chapter 1: Where the Action Is

4. Janet Guthrie, telephone interview with author, August 19, 2009.

5. Guthrie, telephone interview with author.

6. Janet Guthrie, *Janet Guthrie: A Life at Full Throttle*. Toronto, Canada: Sports Media, 2005, p. 65.

7. Guthrie, telephone interview with author.

8. Guthrie, telephone interview with author.

9. Quoted in Gale Biography Resource Center, "Janet Guthrie," Gale Biography Resource Center, Farmington Hills, MI: Gale Group, 1999, http://galenet.galegroup.com/servlet/BioRC.

Chapter 2: Fast and Ferocious

10. Guthrie, telephone interview with author.
11. Guthrie, *Janet Guthrie*, p. 72.
12. Quoted in David Kindred, "Gumption Is as Attractive as Beauty," *Sporting News*, June 17, 2005, p. 56.
13. Guthrie, *Janet Guthrie*, p. 83.

Chapter 3: Running on Empty

14. Guthrie, telephone interview with author.
15. Guthrie, telephone interview with author.
16. Guthrie, *Janet Guthrie*, p. 110.
17. Quoted in Phil Roberts, "NASCAR Female Drivers—One Step at a Time," Stock Car Racing, www.stockcarracing.com/featurestories/scrp_0604_nascar_female_drivers/janet_guthrie.html.
18. Guthrie, *Janet Guthrie*, p. 141.
19. Guthrie, telephone interview with author.

Chapter 4: NASCAR, Indy, and Beyond

20. Guthrie, telephone interview with author.
21. Quoted in Tom Netherland, "The People's Choice," TriCities.com, August 23, 2009, www2.tricities.com/tri/news/local/article/the_peoples_choice/30989.
22. Janet Guthrie, interview by Steve Inskeep, *Morning Edition*, NPR, May 27, 2005, www.npr.org/templates/story/story.php?storyId=4669148.
23. Soundbite of 1977 Indianapolis 500 quoted in Guthrie, interview by Steve Inskeep.
24. Quoted in George, "Pioneer Janet Guthrie Takes a Victory Lap."

GLOSSARY

banked: An upward slope at the turns on a racetrack.

gymkhanas: Amateur contests of driving skill in which competitors drive between rubber cones.

hill-climbing races: Car races in which drivers compete, one car at a time, on winding mountain roads. The winner is the driver who completes the course the fastest.

NASCAR (The National Association for Stock Car Auto Racing): Organization that sponsors car races in which stock cars are raced on banked oval tracks known as superspeedways.

open-wheel cars: Race cars that have wheels fully outside the body of the car, not in wheel wells like regular cars.

physics: The study of force, motion, matter, and energy.

pits: Areas at a racetrack where crews of mechanics refuel, change tires, repair, and adjust race cars.

qualify: To earn a position in a race.

rip cord: A device on a parachute that when pulled causes the parachute to open.

solo: To fly a plane without another pilot present.

stock cars: Standard passenger cars that are modified for professional racing.

superspeedways: Banked oval racetracks at least 1 mile (1.6km) around.

For Further Exploration

Books

Michael Benson, *Women in Racing*. New York: Chelsea House, 1997. This book discusses famous women in car racing, including Janet Guthrie.

James Buckley, *Nascar*. New York: DK, 2005. This book contains all sorts of information about NASCAR racing with lots of pictures.

Matt Doeden, *Sports Car Racing*. Minneapolis, MN: Lerner, 2009. This book offers information about how sports car racing began, the different types of sports car racing, and sports car racetracks.

Ross R. Olney, *Janet Guthrie First Woman at Indy*. New York: Harvey House, 1978. This book discusses Guthrie's life through the 1978 Indy 500.

Janet Piehl, *Indy Race Cars*. Minneapolis, MN: Lerner, 2007. This book provides a look at Indy race cars, how they work, and their history.

Internet Source

Menstuff, "Janet Guthrie," Menstuff, www.menstuff.org/archives/guthrie.html.

Periodical

Nate Ryan, "Female Racing Milestones," USA Today, April 21, 2008.

Web Sites

Indianapolis 500 (www.indy500.com). This is the official Web site of the Indianapolis 500 with information about the race and current drivers.

Janet Guthrie—Racing Legend (www.janetguthrie.com). This is Janet Guthrie's official Web site. It offers pictures, information about her life, excerpts from her book, her career stats, links, and contact information.

INDEX

PICTURE CREDITS

ABOUT THE AUTHOR

Barbara Sheen is the author of more than 50 books for young people. She lives in New Mexico with her family. In her spare time, she likes to swim, cook, and garden. She is inspired and awed by Janet Guthrie and thanks her for the help she gave with this book.

DISCARD